W9-BLA-313

ANCIENT CIVILIZATIONS

ANCIENT GREECE

COLIN HYNSON

WORLD ALMANAC® LIBRARY

Please visit our web site at: www.worldalmaclibrary.com
For a free color catalog describing World Almanac® Library's list of high-quality books
and multimedia programs, call 1-800-848-2928 (USA) or 1-800-387-3178 (Canada).
World Almanac® Library's fax: (414) 332-3567.

Library of Congress Cataloging-in-Publication Data

Hynson, Colin.
    Ancient Greece / by Colin Hynson.
      p. cm. — (Ancient civilizations)
    Includes bibliographical references and index.
    ISBN 0-8368-6190-6 (lib. bdg.)
    1. Greece—Civilization—To 146 B.C.—Juvenile literature. I. Title.
  DF77.H945   2006
  938—dc22   2005051695

This North American edition first published in 2006 by
World Almanac® Library
A Member of the WRC Media Family of Companies
330 West Olive Street, Suite 100
Milwaukee, WI 53212 USA

This U.S. edition copyright © 2006 by World Almanac® Library. Original edition
copyright © 2006 by Hodder Wayland. First published in 2006 by Hodder Wayland,
an imprint of Hodder Children's Books, a division of Hodder Headline Limited,
338 Euston Road, London NW1 3BH, U.K.

Project editor: Kirsty Hamilton
Designer: Simon Borrough
Maps: Peter Bull
World Almanac® Library editor: Gini Holland
World Almanac® Library art direction: Tammy West
World Almanac® Library cover design: Dave Kowalski
World Almanac® Library production: Jessica Morris

Picture credits: The Art Archive / Archaeological Museum Volos / Dagli Orti: Title page, p. 20; Araldo de
Luca / Corbis: pp. 3, 7, 14 , 40 (top); Buddy Mays / Corbis: p. 4; Corbis: p. 9, 42; The Art Archive / Dagli
Orti: pp. 6, 8, 26, 36, 39; Gianni Dagli Orti / Corbis: pp. 10, 13, 19, 37; Topfoto.co.uk: pp. 11, 23, 30;
Christie's Images / Corbis: p. 12; David Forman / Corbis: p. 15; TopFoto.co.uk © The British Museum
/HIP: pp.16, 22, 37; Sandro Vannini / Corbis: pp. 8, 37 (right); TopFoto.co.uk HIP / Ann Ronan Picture
Library: p. 21 (left); The Art Archive / Kanellopoulos Museum Athens / Dagli Orti: p. 21 (right); Archivo
Iconografico, S.A / Corbis: p. 24, 34; Mimmo Jodice / Corbis: pp. 25, 35; The Art Archive / Museo
Nazionale Taranto / Dagli Orti: p. 27; TopFoto.co.uk © Collection Roger-Viollet: pp. 28, 33; Werner
Forman / Corbis: p. 29; Kevin Schafer / Corbis: p. 31; The Art Archive / Musée du Louvre Paris / Dagli
Orti: p. 32; Bettmann / Corbis: p. 37 (left), 38; Kevin Fleming / Corbis: p. 40 (bottom); George Tatge Luca
della Robbia / Corbis: p.41; Jon Hicks / Corbis:pp. 43, 44 (right); William Manning / Corbis: p. 44 (left);
Mike Blake / Corbis: p. 45

Printed in China

1 2 3 4 5 6 7 8 9 10 09 08 07 06

CONTENTS

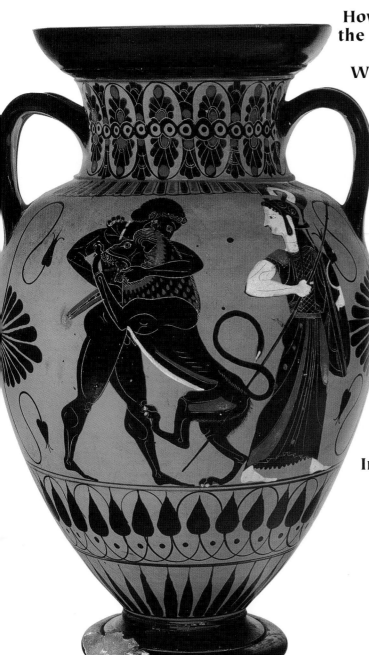

◆◇◆◇◆◇◆◇◆◇◆◇◆◇◆

WHO WERE THE ANCIENT GREEKS?

THE INFLUENCE OF THE ANCIENT GREEKS

Everywhere we look we can see the influence ancient Greece still has on Western culture today. The designs of many famous buildings, the mathematics that we learn in school, the classic plays put on in many theaters, and even the way that many democratic countries choose government leaders—all can be traced back to the ancient Greeks.

One of the main reasons people today know so much about the ancient Greeks—and why their civilization still affects the modern world—is because, in 146 A.D., the Romans conquered them. The Romans then adopted much of Greek culture and made it their own. As the Roman Empire spread, Romans took their love of all things Greek with them. When the Roman Empire fell, the ancient Greeks soon were forgotten. Centuries later, Muslim scholars discovered the Greeks. Contact between Muslims and the West eventually brought knowledge of Greek civilization back to Europe.

The Palace of Knossos

What does it tell us?

Ancient Greece was strongly influenced by the Minoans. It was only in the early twentieth century that the ancient Minoan civilization (*see page 6*) was discovered. British archaeologist Arthur Evans became interested in some mysterious coins and seals found in Crete and he visited the island to see what else he could find. Between 1900 and 1906, he discovered and excavated a four-story building, part of the palace of Knossos (*shown below*). His excavation provided much of the evidence we have of the Minoans. Evans rebuilt part of the palace to show what it had looked like: Many archaeologists think he should have left it as found.

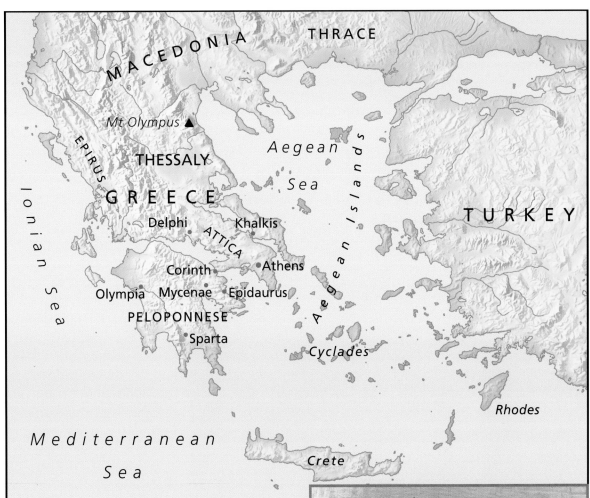

The map labels, reading across the image:

MACEDONIA   THRACE

Mt Olympus ▲

EPIRUS

THESSALY

Aegean

Sea

GREECE

Delphi   Khalkis

ATTICA

Aegean Islands

TURKEY

Corinth   Athens

Olympia   Mycenae   Epidaurus

Ionian Sea

PELOPONNESE

Sparta

Cyclades

Rhodes

Mediterranean

Sea

Crete

THE ANCIENT GREEK WORLD

Greece lies in the Mediterranean Sea and forms part of the border of southern Europe. It is made up of the mainland and a large number of islands in the Ionian and Aegean Seas. The largest islands include Crete and Rhodes.

Greece is a mountainous country, and good farming land is in short supply. The dry, hot summers and wet winters made growing crops even more difficult for the ancient Greeks. This scarcity of

Map of ancient Greece

What does it tell us?

This map shows ancient Greece (c. 650–30 B.C.) and its colonies around the Mediterranean Sea. The ancient Greeks built towns and cities but also traveled east and founded colonies in an area known as Ionia (modern Turkey). The fact that they built Greek cities outside Greece tells us that, as Greece became prosperous and its population grew, the country probably needed more land for agriculture and living space.

Lion gate of Mycenae

What does it tell us?

The Mycenaean civilization took its name from the city of Mycenae. This lion gate was built about 1250 B.C. It is much wider and more richly decorated than the other entrances to the city. The gate is wide enough to allow carts to pass through it. Carved above it are two lions, the symbol of the Mycenaean royal family. These features reveal how important this particular gate was to the Mycenaeans and that it was probably the main entrance through the city walls.

good soil for growing food meant that people had to gather together to protect what good land was under their control. By the middle of the eighth century B.C., these small communities began to transform themselves into city-states. These were cities that controlled large areas of land around them. The main city-states were Athens and Sparta. Smaller city-states included Thebes and the island of Naxos. Each of these city-states developed their own way of ruling themselves and created their own leaders.

WHAT CAME BEFORE THE ANCIENT GREEKS?

The great achievements of the ancient Greeks were influenced by earlier civilizations that had arisen in Greece. The island of Crete was home to one of the earliest civilizations, known as the Minoans. The Minoans were at their most powerful between 2200 B.C. and 1400 B.C. They built many rich palaces that were funded by trading around the Mediterranean. The palace of Knossos is the best known of the Minoan palaces.

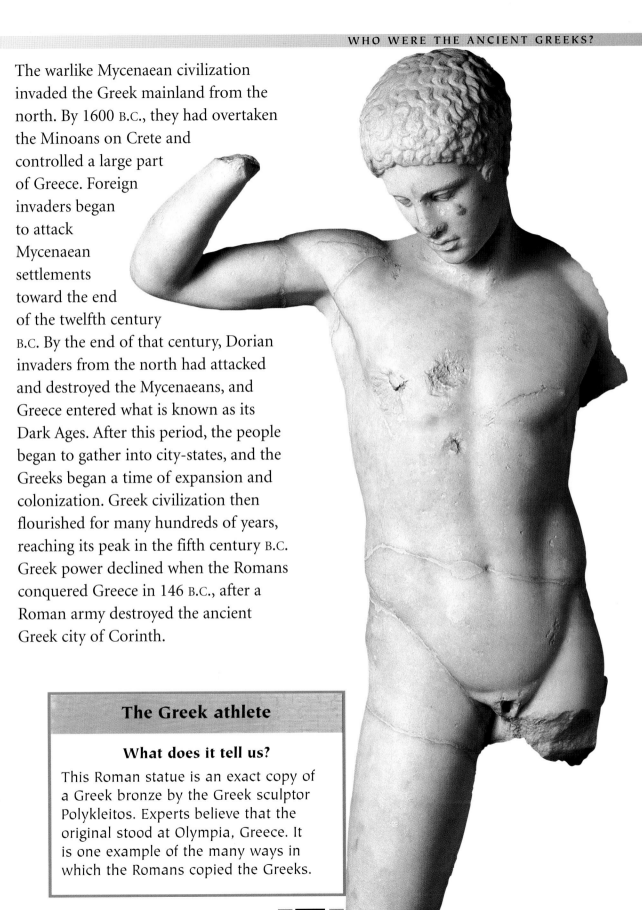

The warlike Mycenaean civilization invaded the Greek mainland from the north. By 1600 B.C., they had overtaken the Minoans on Crete and controlled a large part of Greece. Foreign invaders began to attack Mycenaean settlements toward the end of the twelfth century B.C. By the end of that century, Dorian invaders from the north had attacked and destroyed the Mycenaeans, and Greece entered what is known as its Dark Ages. After this period, the people began to gather into city-states, and the Greeks began a time of expansion and colonization. Greek civilization then flourished for many hundreds of years, reaching its peak in the fifth century B.C. Greek power declined when the Romans conquered Greece in 146 B.C., after a Roman army destroyed the ancient Greek city of Corinth.

The Greek athlete

What does it tell us?

This Roman statue is an exact copy of a Greek bronze by the Greek sculptor Polykleitos. Experts believe that the original stood at Olympia, Greece. It is one example of the many ways in which the Romans copied the Greeks.

HOW DID THE GREEKS RULE THEMSELVES?

B y the eighth century B.C., the Greeks emerged from their dark ages and began to create the Greek civilization that has left such a great impact on today's world. At this time, however, ancient Greece was not a single, unified country like modern Greece. It was a region made up of different city-states. City-states were large areas of land that were dominated by a city. The best-known city-states were Athens and Sparta. These city-states usually coexisted peacefully, but they were rivals, and occasionally, conflicts arose between them.

THE RISE OF ATHENS

The most important of the city-states in ancient Greece was Athens. Between 490 and 479 B.C., the Greeks were involved in fighting a war against the Persians, who came from the area known today as Iran. In 480 B.C., the Persians attacked Athens and destroyed the temples on the Acropolis, a collection of important buildings situated on a hill looking over the city. Led by the Athenians, the Greeks defeated the Persians in 490 B.C. This victory allowed Athens to become a great power within Greece. The Athenian leader, Pericles, ordered a huge rebuilding program of the temples that were destroyed. In the era after the war, Athens became an important center of commerce, learning, literature, and the arts. Athens's economic success was due to the trade that came through Piraeus, its nearby port.

Athena's temple: the Parthenon

What does it tell us?

Historians can tell how important a building is by looking at its size, its location, and the materials used to make it. The Parthenon was dedicated to the goddess Athena. It was built on a hill, the Acropolis, in a central part of Athens, in 447–438 B.C. Built entirely of marble, it served as a focus for the political life of the Athenians.

SPARTA—ATHENS'S RIVAL

The other main city-state in Greece was Sparta. Founded in the tenth century B.C. by the Dorians, Sparta became, by the seventh century B.C., similar to Athens in many ways—especially in art and literature. During the sixth century B.C., however, defeat in war by the Messenians convinced the Spartans that, in order to survive, they had to become more disciplined and have a stronger military.

The army soon became the most important section of Spartan society. At the age of seven, Spartan boys were taken from their families to live in army barracks. They then began a program of military training called the *agoge*, which included being regularly beaten to toughen them up. In this way, the Spartans created one of the most feared armies in the Greek world. Spartan girls also were trained to become fit and strong, but only so that they could have healthy babies who would then grow up to serve in the Spartan army. Marriage was permitted from the age of twenty, but husbands could not live with their wives until they were thirty years old.

Ruins of the city of Sparta

What does it tell us?

Very little is left of the ancient city of Sparta. It was actually four villages around the Eurotas River. No city wall existed, which shows us that the Spartans were confident in the power of their army. They must have felt that they did not need a wall to defend themselves, but they were destroyed by the Goths in 396 B.C.

ATHENS—RULE BY THE PEOPLE?

When the city-states began to arise in Greece, they were controlled by their most powerful and wealthy families. Several city-states, including Athens, experienced struggles between these families and the people over whom they ruled. By the middle of the sixth century B.C., the people of Athens won their struggle and created a new form of government called *democracy*.

The most important body in this new form of government was called the Assembly. The Assembly was a gathering of the citizens of Athens who made all of the major decisions that affected the city-state. Every citizen could speak and vote at the Assembly. At least six thousand citizens had to be present before any decisions could be made. The Assembly met on a hill near the Acropolis called the Pnyx. The

Voting in Athens

What does it tell us?

We know little about how Athenian citizens debated and voted. Greek writers mention that members were voted off the Assembly by having their names scratched onto a bit of pottery, like the one in the picture. The votes were then gathered together in a large jar and counted.

Assembly's business was controlled by a group of five hundred citizens who met in a building called the *tholos*.

Although this government appears to be a democratic system, only the free men of Athens could take part in making decisions. Therefore, many people in Athens—including women and slaves—had no right to join the Assembly.

SPARTA—A STRICT GOVERNMENT

Sparta had an unusual system of government. The Spartans had a monarchy. but there always were two kings at the same time. This meant the power had to be shared. Below the two kings was a council of twenty-eight nobles, all of whom had to be over sixty years old. The council decided the policies of Sparta and was selected by an Assembly of Spartan males. The council was controlled by a small group of five men called the *ephorate,* also elected by the assembly. The ephors also controlled the army and decided on the system of education. They could veto anything the council decided on. The ephorate even had the right to overthrow a monarch.

Quote from Thucydides (460–400 B.C.)

"After this speech, Sthenelaidas himself, as ephor, put the question to the Spartan Assembly. They actually made their decisions by shouting and not by voting."

What does it tell us?

This short piece tells us that the Spartan Assembly's way of coming to a decision was different from the Athenian way of voting. Some historians view this way of deciding as less democratic because it was not secret.

The remains of the *tholos* on a hill called the Pnyx, near Athens, where the business of the Assembly was conducted. ▼

HOW LARGE WAS THE GREEK EMPIRE?

B efore 1000 B.C., a Greek Empire did not exist. After that date, a rapidly growing population in Greece meant that new living space had to be found. Many Greeks left their homes to found new colonies around the Mediterranean. These new Greek communities could be found in what are now modern-day Turkey, Italy, Tunisia, and Cyprus. They did not conquer these lands but simply settled there. It was only with their Macedonian conqueror, Alexander the Great, in the fourth century B.C., that the Greeks began to create an empire.

THE GREEK ARMY

Even before the military campaigns of Alexander the Great, the Greek city-states needed armies to defend themselves and their colonies from outside attack. In every city-state, it was expected that all men would train to fight in the army. In many cases, soldiers had to buy their own armor and equipment. In Athens, young men were trained as soldiers for two years after they reached their eighteenth birthday. Military training in Sparta started even at seven and was far more harsh.

Bronze helmet

What does it tell us?

This helmet comes from Corinth and dates from around 460 B.C. It is made of bronze, which was a very expensive material. It was also shaped from just one piece of bronze, which would have needed a lot of skill and time from the metalworker. This suggests that only some Greeks were able to afford this kind of protection when fighting. The helmet also shows us how fully some soldiers were protected in battle.

THE SOLDIER

Infantry soldiers were the backbone of all the ancinet Greek armies. They were trained to fight in close formations called *phalanxes.* Well-armed Greek soldiers were called *hoplites.* This came from *hoplon,* which meant "shield." Not all soldiers had a shield because some could not afford to buy one. Only wealthy families could afford to protect their sons by buying them a shield, helmet, and armor.

Dressing for battle

"Regarding their equipment for battle, Lykourgos (a Spartan lawgiver from about 700 B.C.) devised that they should have a crimson cloak and a bronze shield . . . He also allowed those who reached adulthood to wear their hair long, considering that they would look taller, more noble, and more terrifying."

What does it tell us?

This quote from the ancient Greek historian Xenophon (430–355 B.C.) tells us something about what the Spartan warriors looked like when dressed for battle. It also tells us that the Spartans believed that it was important that their soldiers appear to be strong. The crimson cloak was the warlike color of blood. This may have made the soldiers appear more fearsome and awe-inspiring.

The armor usually was made of strong bronze, but the round, convex shield often was made of wood. The breastplate, which protected the upper body, was made to fit the individual soldier. This custom tailoring was a very expensive way of being protected. Hoplites also could have bronze leg guards, called greaves. These protected the soldiers' vulnerable lower legs during battle.

◀ This late fourth-century B.C. Hellenistic painting shows a hoplite warrior in battle dress.

ALEXANDER THE GREAT

The military strength of ancient Greece became even more important when a twenty year-old man became ruler of Macedonia, a state bordering ancient Greece to the north, in 337 B.C. His name was Alexander, and he was soon to be known as Alexander the Great. His father, King Philip II, had subdued every Greek city-state and made Macedonia the head of a new and powerful Greece.

When Alexander became leader of Macedonia, he had to face a rebellion. He crushed the rebels without mercy and executed anybody who appeared to be a threat to his position. He began to believe that Macedonia and the rest of Greece would not be safe until the Persians, the main enemy of Greece, had been subdued.

A man of action

What does it tell us?

This image of Alexander the Great shows him fighting the Persian king Darius III at the battle of Issos (333 B.C.). Along with many other sources, this image shows that Alexander the Great was viewed as a brave soldier who took an active part in fighting during battles.

THE EMPIRE BEGINS

In 334 B.C., Alexander launched an attack on the Persians. He advanced through modern-day Turkey, Syria, Lebanon, and Israel. His army then conquered Egypt. In 333 B.C., he defeated the main Persian army under King Darius III at Issus, which is in modern-day Syria. Alexander then carried on through Syria and what is called Iraq today. In 331 B.C., his army met Darius's army again near the city of

Babylon. Again, Alexander defeated Darius's army, leaving the Persian Empire defenseless.

THE END OF EMPIRE

In the winter of 331 B.C., Alexander took Persepolis, the capital of the Persian Empire (in present-day Iran). He ordered the city to be looted and destroyed. He continued to march eastward while pushing the Persian army to one side. By 327 B.C., he controlled much of what is now called Central Asia. In 326 B.C., his army crossed the Indus River and began to march through India. At this point, his advance came to a halt when his soldiers simply refused to go any farther. He returned to Babylon in 323 B.C. and died of a fever.

THE INFLUENCE OF ALEXANDER

Alexander had built one of the greatest empires the world has ever seen. He controlled large parts of the Mediterranean, Asia, and India. In this way, his new Empire spread Greek culture and ideas beyond the borders of Greece. He began a new period of Greek history, which is called the Hellenistic Age. The name comes from the Greek word, *Helles*, which means Greece. For much of the Mediterranean area and Asia, this was the Greek Age. It was only when the Romans conquered the Greeks, about two hundred years later, that the Hellenistic Age came to an end.

The ruins of Pergamum

What does it tell us?

The ruined city of Pergamum (*shown below*), in modern-day Turkey, could be mistaken for a ruined ancient city in modern Greece because the style of the buildings are the same. Alexander the Great built several cities, and all of them resembled Greek cities. These cities were meant to show local populations that Greece was meant to last. The cities also had a defensive job and were used to control their surrounding areas.

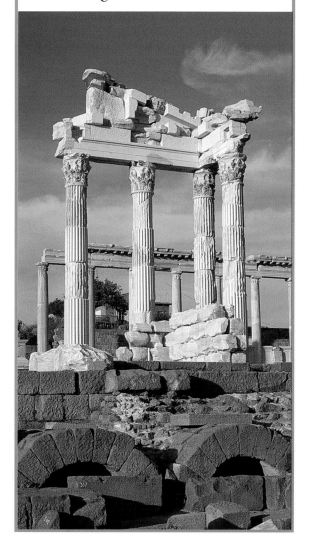

WHAT WAS LIFE LIKE FOR THE ANCIENT GREEKS?

ANCIENT GREEK CLOTHING

Ancient Greek clothing and fashion changed very little over hundreds of years. Everybody was expected to wear the same style of clothing. Any attempt to put on something a little different was disapproved of. There also was not much difference between the clothing of men and women, adults and children, or rich and poor. For everyone, the basic piece of clothing was a tunic that was fastened with a brooch, and a cloak thrown over the top. There were, however, some differences in the kinds of clothes the ancient Greeks wore.

Most clothing was made from the wool of local sheep. As the ancient Greeks improved the way this wool was spun, they were able to make it thinner and more comfortable. In the middle of the sixth century B.C., the wool began to be replaced with linen, which is woven from flax plants. This linen was much smoother and lighter to wear. The wealthiest people could afford to buy silk from merchants in the Middle East. The Greeks started making their own silk in the fourth century B.C.

WOMEN'S CLOTHING

In the eighth century B.C., the women of Athens wore a *peplos*. This was a long,

Terra-cotta "Tanagra" figure

What does it tell us?

This figure comes from a site in central Greece that was unearthed in the 1870s. Thousands of little figures like this one were found. These figures helped historians learn more about Greek clothing. This female figure is wearing a *chiton* and a *himation*. Traces of paint tell us about the color of these clothes.

heavy, woolen, sleeveless garment that was secured with two large pins at the shoulders and a belt around the waist. It was usually plain but dyed purple. By the middle of the sixth century B.C., this began to be replaced by the *chiton*. The chiton was made of linen and was lighter and finer than the peplos. The chiton had loose sleeves and was held in place with a belt and pins along the sleeves. The peplos remained popular in other parts of Greece, particularly where the weather was colder.

MEN'S CLOTHING

For some men, the most basic piece of clothing was a short tunic called an *exomis*. This tunic just about covered the knees and was worn by workmen and slaves. Men also could wear a chiton and a rectangular piece of cloth, also worn by women, called a *himation*. This cloth was draped over the left shoulder and hung over the right arm.

LIVING AT HOME

The homes of ordinary ancient Greeks have disappeared. Unlike the great temples, they were not built of strong materials and were not made to last. This means that there is very little evidence of the home life of many ancient Greeks. Enough remains of the houses of some wealthier people, however, to give some idea of the typical construction and layout.

The Spartans were first

"The Spartans were the first to adopt a moderate costume . . . and in other respects too, the propertied class of Athens changed their way of life to correspond as closely as possible to that of ordinary men."

What does it tell us?

This quote, from the ancient Greek historian, Thucydides, tells us that men wanted to dress as plainly and simply as possible. A man wearing plain clothing was seen as virtuous. Bright clothes that attracted attention were considered a sign of vanity and arrogance.

BUILDING MATERIALS

The Greeks built most of their houses with sun-dried mud bricks coated with lime. These were not very strong and could be washed away in a storm. One ancient Greek word for burglar means "wall-breaker," which suggests it was fairly easy to smash a hole in an ancient Greek house. Greeks also made their interior walls of this brick and sometimes added a layer of plaster that could be painted and decorated. Floors usually were beaten earth or clay. From the fourth century B.C., Greeks began to decorate their floors with mosaics.

▲ This A.D. second–third century bas-relief sculpture shows Hermes, the protector of boundaries.

THE LAYOUT OF THE HOUSE

Many Greeks built their houses around an open courtyard or garden. All of the main rooms in the house faced this courtyard. The homes had only small windows in each room, and they would be set up high in the wall. This provided protection from the weather. On the porch they placed a *Herm*, a small statue of the god Hermes, which they set there to protect the home from evil spirits. Greeks also set up an altar in the house where the family could worship together.

In many houses, men and women had their own areas, where they slept, ate, worked, and entertained. The women's part of the house was known as the *gynaeceum*. It usually was placed at the back of the house so that the women had as much privacy as possible. The men had an area known as the *andron*. This area usually was used to feed and entertain friends and could be found on the north side of the courtyard so that it could catch the winter sun.

UNIQUE GREEK POTTERY

It was well-known that the best pottery in ancient Greek homes came from Athens. This pottery was preferred

Ancient Greek loom weights

What does it tell us?

Loom weights (*shown below*) were used in weaving clothes. Many of the loom weights found in the ruins of ancient Greece were near the sites of houses. This tells us that much of the weaving was done inside the home rather than in separate workshops.

because the local clay would turn into an attractive reddish-brown color after it was fired. Athens had an area known as the *Kerameikos,* where many of the potters worked. Experts estimate that in the fifth century B.C. there were about five hundred potters working at any one time. These potters produced large quantities of pottery that found its way to every part of the Greek world. Pottery designs changed over the centuries. From the tenth to the seventh centuries B.C., geometric patterns were dominant. In the sixth century B.C., Greek potters began to paint black figures onto the reddish-brown backgrounds. From about 500 B.C., they reversed this, so that the background was black and their pictures emerged as reddish-brown.

JEWELRY

Jewelry was an important way for ancient Greek women to show their wealth and importance. The city-state of Corinth became well-known for the quality of its metalwork. The jewelry was made by skilled craftsmen using a variety of materials. The jewelers' most common materials were painted terra-cotta, copper, and lead. The most wealthy could afford silver and gold. Men wore only one piece of jewelry: a small signet ring. Men often used their rings—usually topped with a flat disk decorated with an initial or design on top—to press their seals onto documents and merchandise.

GROWING UP IN ANCIENT GREECE: CHILDHOOD YEARS

Newborn babies in ancient Greece were only officially part of a family five days after birth. On that day, the family performed the ceremony of *Amphidromia* at the hearth of the house. The father would hold the baby and carry his infant around the hearth. He would dedicate the baby to the goddess Hestia. Babies were then named on their tenth day. First-born boys were given their grandfather's name. Some babies were not so welcome. In Sparta, every newborn baby was brought by the father to the ruling council. If it was healthy, it was taken away to be brought up to serve Sparta. If it was decided that the baby was weak or sick, it was taken to the foot of a nearby mountain and left to die.

When Athenian children reached four years of age, they took part in the *Anthesteria*, or Flower Festival. They each were given a wreath of flowers to wear and a small jug called a *chouse*. This was also the time when children had their first taste of wine. It was a sign that they were no longer babies.

GOING TO SCHOOL

In Sparta, boys were removed from their families at age seven and were trained to become soldiers. They could not live in their own homes until they were thirty. In many other parts of ancient Greece, the boys of wealthy parents went to school at seven years of age. Teachers, called *grammatistes*, taught their students reading, arithmetic, and writing. Pupils

---

Golden wreath

What does it tell us?

This wreath shows us how skilled ancient Greek craftsmen were in working with gold. Greeks placed golden wreaths such as this on the heads of statues of goddesses and gods. They also have been found in the graves of ancient Greek women.

---

also had to learn poetry and to play a musical instrument. Girls did not go to school but sometimes had private tutors. Girls of all economic classes usually were taught by their mothers about how to run a home.

PLAYING GAMES

Ancient Greek children did have some time to play games. For example, knucklebone was a popular children's game. Players competed by throwing pieces of bone in the air and catching

Clay toys

What does it tell us?

Archaeologists have not found many ancient Greek toys, probably because they usually were made of materials such as cloth, which does not survive very well. Also, ancient Greek children did not have as many toys as children do today. This terra-cotta toy warrior, from the eleventh century B.C., has survived intact. The warrior is carrying a lance and is riding a horse on wheels. The child would have pushed or pulled the toy along.

Greek boy reads to a tutor

What does it tell us?

This scene from a vessel shows pupils at an Athenian school. A tutor holds a scroll that a boy is reading. It shows us, among other things, that wealthy boys who went to school usually stood during lessons.

them on the backs of their hands. Many children also played a board game similar to checkers.

Children played with homemade toys, and because they usually were made from wood and linen, few of them have survived to the present day. Dolls with

movable arms and legs were popular, along with clay figures of animals. Only children of wealthy parents had toys.

THE STATUS OF WOMEN IN ANCIENT GREECE

The lives of girls and women in ancient Greece were much more restricted than those of boys and men. Women were not allowed to take part in any of the decisions of the city-state in which they lived. Girls were not educated in the same way as boys and they usually were taught only how to run a home properly. On top of that, women were not supposed to inherit or own property, particularly once they were married.

GETTING MARRIED

Women did not choose their husbands. The marriage of a couple usually was the result of discussions between the fathers

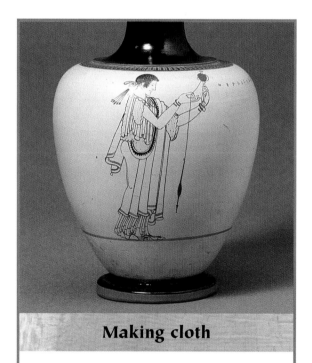

Making cloth

What does it tell us?
The picture on this ancient Greek vase portrays a woman in the act of spinning thread. This illustration shows how women spun wool into thread with a drop spindle. They then wove the thread into cloth.

Advice for women

"You must stay indoors and send out the slaves whose work is outside. Those who remain and do chores inside the house are under your charge. You are to inspect everything that enters it . . . taking care not to be extravagant."

What does it tell us?
This advice came from a book called *Household Management,* written by Xenophon in the fourth century B.C. It tells us that the ancient Greeks believed the main duties of the wife were to stay indoors and to look after the house and servants.

of the man and woman. Ancient Greeks considered it normal for a woman to marry when she was about thirteen or fourteen years old. Her husband usually was much older, so it was common for a woman to become a widow by the time she had reached thirty years old.

A WOMAN'S DUTY

As soon as a woman was married, her duty was to have children, especially boys. Historians believe that many more Spartan baby girls were left to die than boys. Apart from bringing up children, women also were expected to look after the affairs of the home. If they had slaves, a woman's duty meant making sure that the slaves were doing their jobs. If they did not have any slaves, then the women had to do the work themselves. Spinning and weaving were seen as important tasks for women because ancient Greek women made many of the clothes worn by all members of their family.

A FEMALE POET

Very little is known about individual ancient Greek women. One woman we do know something about is Sappho (650–590 B.C.). Sappho was born on the island of Lesbos, where women were given more freedom than on the Greek mainland. She was born into a noble family, was married, and had one daughter. She is most famous for a series of poems that she wrote with a group of other women and for creating a new kind of poetry called *Sapphics*. Many later ancient Greek writers, such as Plato and Theocritus, were influenced by her work.

FOOD AND FEASTING

One of the tasks women had at home was to cook and prepare food. Food was very important to the ancient Greeks. Eating and drinking were not just essential for their health, but they also were an important part of their social and religious lives. The people of Athens usually had two meals a day. The first was a light lunch called *ariston*. The second, main meal—called *deipnon*—was served in the evening. Wealthy Greeks ate while reclining on a couch, and they usually picked up their food with their fingers. When slaves prepared

the food, they had to cut it before they served it, so that their masters could pick the food up easily. Both wealthy and ordinary ancient Greeks used flat bread as a kind of spoon.

THE FOOD OF THE GREEKS

The food that the ancient Greeks ate usually was very simple. Because Greece is surrounded on three sides by seas, food from the sea was important in the ancient Greek diet. Octopus and squid

Picking olives

What does it tell us?

This fifth-century vase painting shows some men knocking down and gathering olives. This scene illustrates how Greeks harvested olives. Olives and olive oil were a central part of the ancient Greek diet. Olive oil also was used by the ancient Greeks to light lamps and to clean themselves.

were plentiful and eaten by most people. Local fishermen sold fish such as tuna, mackerel, and sturgeon, which the women typically cooked on beds of herbs. Ancient Greeks' most common vegetables included carrots, cabbage, and artichokes. They also ate lentils in large quantities and cheese made from the milk of either goats or sheep.

A DRINKING PARTY

Many ancient Greeks drank wine with their meals. They usually diluted the wine with water and sweetened it with honey before drinking it from small plain clay cups. Men drank wine in greater quantities at all-male feasts known as symposiums, which normally took place after the food had been eaten. Symposiums typically were held in the andron of a house. Women usually had to withdraw from these parties, but some were paid to play music and dance for the men. The men started the symposium by drinking a toast to Zeus and other gods and goddesses.

THE OLYMPIC GAMES

The ancient Greeks believed that sport was important as a way of honoring the gods, celebrating the greatness of the city-states, and training for warfare. The Greeks held hundreds of athletic festivals throughout Greece. Their most important were the all-Greek games. These were named the *Nemean, Pythian, Isthmian,* and Olympic games. Each of these games was part of a religious festival dedicated to a god or goddess. The most famous of these games were the Olympic Games held at Olympia. The games were dedicated to the god Zeus.

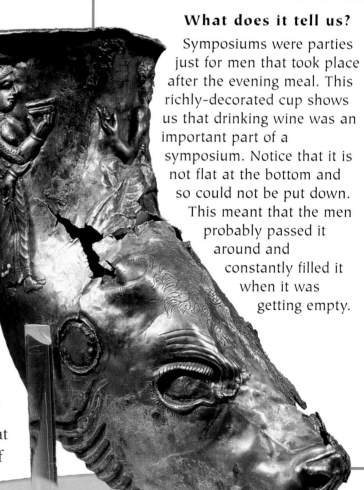

Symposium drinking cup

What does it tell us?

Symposiums were parties just for men that took place after the evening meal. This richly-decorated cup shows us that drinking wine was an important part of a symposium. Notice that it is not flat at the bottom and so could not be put down. This meant that the men probably passed it around and constantly filled it when it was getting empty.

The sport of diving

What does it tell us?

This image was painted on the inside of the lid of a tomb and dates from about 480 B.C. It shows a naked boy diving off a specially built board into some water. Although diving was not part of the Olympic festival, the fact that special diving boards were built shows that this probably was a popular pastime in ancient Greece.

The first recorded Olympic Games were held in 776 B.C., when an official list of all the competitors was compiled. The games took place every four years until 261 B.C. The Greeks did not cancel the games once in all that time. They suspended all wars between city-states during the games and allowed everybody to travel safely to and from Olympia. By 472 B.C., the games had expanded from a one-day event into a festival five days long. Large crowds gathered to watch the games.

THE ATHLETICS

On the first day of the Olympics, the participants took oaths, said prayers, and made sacrifices. The highlight of their second day was a chariot race that took place in a stadium called a *hippodrome*. The pentathlon took place after the chariot race. The Olympic Games dedicated the afternoon of the third day

Losing at the Olympics

"They, when their mothers meet them, have no sweet laughter around them, arousing delight. But in back streets they cower . . . bitten by disaster."

What does it tell us?

This extract from Pindar (518–438 B.C.) tells that while victors in the Olympics were covered in glory, the athletes who lost also brought shame upon themselves and probably on their families and city-states as well.

to sports for young men between the ages of twelve and eighteen. On the fourth day, the athletics took place in the morning, and field sports took place in the afternoon. On the fifth day, the winners received laurel wreaths. Victors were given lavish feasts when they returned home. The city-states with the most winners gained a great deal of prestige.

The modern, international Olympic Games were inspired by these ancient games. The first of the modern Olympic Games was held in Athens in 1896. They have been held almost every four years ever since. Unlike the ancient Greeks, modern countries occasionally have suspended them during times of war.

GREEK DRAMA

As well as the spectacle of sports, the ancient Greeks also gathered for entertainment at the theater. Greek theater can be traced back to Athens and the tyrant Peisistratos in the sixth century B.C. He started a new festival in honor of

Dionysus, the god of drama, dancing, and wine, in which plays were put on as a competition. By the fifth century B.C., actors performed both tragedies and comedies. Women were not allowed to act and, therefore, men always played the female parts.

Epidauros

What does it tell us?

This theater in Epidauros is one of the best-preserved in Greece. The remains of other theaters exist throughout Greece. Many of them could hold fourteen thousand people—or more. The size of the theater tells us just how important theater was to the ancient Greeks, especially during religious festivals when many dramas were enacted.

A Greek comedy

What does it tell us?

This vase painting shows a scene from a comedy. The actors wear strange masks and have padding in their clothes to make them appear fatter. This scene tells us that Greek plays did not always deal with serious subjects and that audiences at the theaters also wanted to laugh.

GREEK THEATERS

A Greek theater consisted of a space called a *theatron*, which is where the audience sat, and a circular *orchestra*, where the drama took place. In the fifth century B.C., the seats for the audience were wooden, but by the next century stone seats were more common. Playwrights had to put on their plays during the day in order to use the light of the Sun. The actors often expected audiences to watch four or five plays in a row without any intermissions. This sometimes could take ten hours.

Some magnificent ancient Greek theaters have survived to this day. The Theater of Dionysus in Athens could hold about twenty thousand people—about half of the population of ancient Athens. The best-preserved ancient Greek theater, which could seat about fourteen thousand people, is at Epidauros.

GREEK DRAMATISTS

Complete plays by only three ancient Greek dramatists have survived to the present day. The earliest of the three was by Aeschylus (525–456 B.C.). Aeschylus wrote about ninety tragedies, but only seven exist now. He was the first dramatist to introduce dialogue, in which two actors talk to each other on stage. His plays include *Seven Against Thebes*, *Agamemnon*, and *Eumenides*. The next dramatist of the three was Sophocles (495–406 B.C.). Only seven of his plays survive. He introduced a third actor to the dialogue to make what was happening on stage even more complex. His most famous play is *Oedipus the King*. The last great ancient Greek dramatist was Euripides (480–406 B.C.). Nineteen of his plays survive. His plays looked at the effects of war. He got into trouble with the Athenian authorities at times for criticizing religious and political ideas. One of the best-known comic writers was Aristophones (448–385 B.C.). His plays, such as *The Wasps* and *Plutus,* were very popular. His writing has influenced many comic writers in the past five hundred years.

GREEK MUSIC

Music often played an important part in ancient Greek drama and at the drinking parties called symposiums. Music also had a part in the daily lives of the ancient Greeks. Many celebrations such as births, weddings, or funerals included music. The most popular instrument was the lyre, a kind of harp. The most common wind instrument was the *aulos,* which resembled a modern flute.The *salpinx* was the nearest that the ancient Greeks had to a horn.

Dancing usually was performed by the chorus, a group of actors who described the action of the play, in Greek dramas. Greek men did not dance because it was seen as improper for them to do so. Dancing girls were hired to perform for symposiums.

GREEK GAMES

Aside from the athletic Olympic competitions that we think of as the "Greek Games," ancient Greeks often played games of wit, skill, and chance for amusement. Drinking games among the men also were popular. For example, during the wine-drinking at symposiums, the men would take part in various games. One of the most popular was the capping game: The first player would recite a line from a poem and the second had to continue by reciting the

Playing the lyre

What does it tell us?

By looking at images of ancient Greeks playing their instruments, we can learn a lot about their music. We know that women often played musical instruments. This painting on a fifth century B.C. attic bowl shows us how the lyre was held and how the strings were plucked. The woman is holding a plectrum to play the lyre.

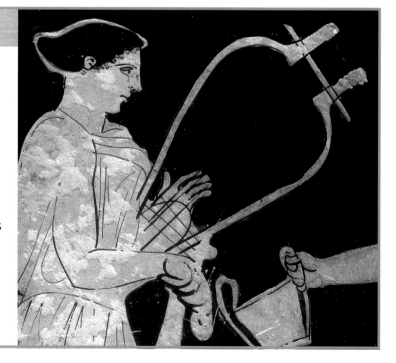

Playing knucklebone

What does it tell us?

Images of people playing a game called knucklebone often appear on vase paintings or as statues (*as shown above*). Most of these images show children and young women playing it. This shows that knucklebone was a very popular game in ancient Greece and that it was seen as suitable for women to play.

next few lines. The men also played a game called *kottabos*: Players would hold their wine cups and flick their wine at a target. The most accurate would be the winner.

Archaeologists have unearthed ample evidence that the ancient Greeks also played board games. Counters, dice, and gaming pieces have been found. They also have found vases with pictures of soldiers playing board games. It appears as though the board games may have been similar to backgammon or checkers. Because many artifacts have survived for thousands of years, we can see how Greeks entertained themselves.

HOW DID THE GREEKS COMMUNICATE?

THE GREEK ALPHABET

So much of what is now known about the ancient Greeks comes from the fact that they had a well-developed alphabet and writing system. The ancient Greeks began writing in the early eighth century B.C. It was at this time that they came into contact with a seafaring people from modern-day Syria called the Phoenicians. The ancient Greeks adapted the Phoenician alphabet to their own language. The Phoenician alphabet had sixteen consonants. The ancient Greeks added seven vowels to this alphabet, which made it easier to represent words. These letters also represented numbers and musical notes.

The earliest known surviving piece of Greek writing dates from about 740 B.C. The different city-states slowly adopted this alphabet until it was standard across the whole region by the beginning of the fourth century B.C.. This standardization of writing and numbers made trade, mathematics, and communication between the city-states much easier.

Reading a papyrus

What does it tell us?

This image shows that some women were taught how to read. These usually were the daughters of the wealthy. The image also shows how a papyrus was rolled up and read. The papyrus scroll was rolled onto a stick or baton at each end and would have to be pulled apart with both hands before it could be read.

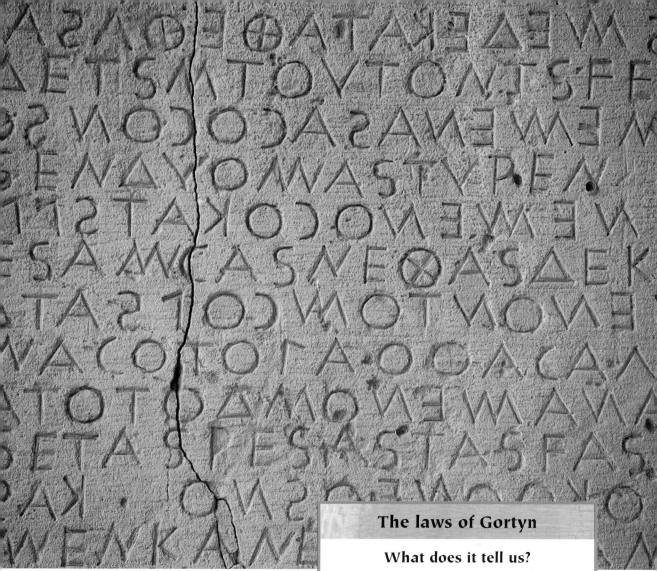

GREEK WRITING

The ancient Greeks wrote mainly on papyrus. This ancient form of paper comes from the papyrus plant that grows in lower Egypt. Leaves from the papyrus plant were laid across each other and then pressed flat so that the leaves were squashed against each other. So, in the same way that the ancient Greeks borrowed their alphabet from the Phoenicians, they also took their writing materials from another culture with which they came into contact.

The laws of Gortyn

What does it tell us?

One of the longest and best-preserved of early Greek inscriptions, the laws of Gortyn—the earliest known Greek legal code—was carved in 450 B.C. (but created as early as the sixth century B.C.) in the town of Gortyna in Crete. This inscription shows how writing in ancient Greece helped the rulers and the ruled communicate and preserve the laws of their civilization.

Book scrolls written on papyrus seemed to be available from about the end of the fifth century B.C. These books were copied by slaves and were inexpensive.

COMMUNICATING ACROSS DISTANCES

A rugged coastline and a mountainous country made ancient Greece a difficult country for outside armies to attack. Unfortunately, its mountains also made it difficult for Greeks to communicate with each other across long distances. Mountains did make it easier for fire and smoke signals to be used because they were high up. Aeschylus wrote in *Agamemnon* that the news of the defeat of Troy by the Greek army was spread by fire signals, which everybody knew in advance would mean victory. Pigeons were also used to send messages. News of victories at the Olympic Games were often sent by pigeon.

Ancient Greek stylus

What does it tell us?

Besides papyrus, ancient Greeks also wrote on wax tablets. These were usually used by children when they were at school. Liquid wax was poured onto a wooden tablet. When the wax hardened, the children could write on it. Students used a stylus to scratch letters into the wax, as shown by this terra-cotta figurine. The styli were made cheaply because they were meant for practice and were used mainly by children.

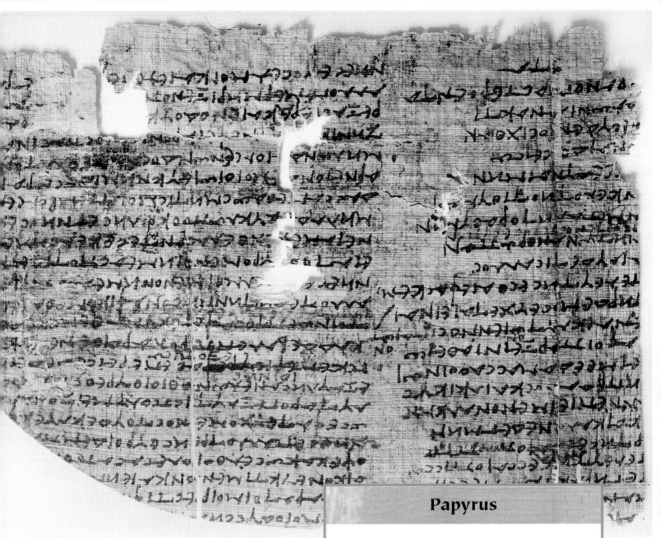

Papyrus

What does it tell us?

This fragment of a papyrus comes from second century A.D. Egypt. It shows part of a play by the Greek writer Sophocles. The condition of the papyrus shows us that papyrus does not survive well and is one reason why so little Greek writing still exists. Sophocles, for example, wrote over one hundred and twenty plays, yet we only have the complete text of seven. The fact that this papyrus was found in Egypt shows that written work spread to other countries.

The most common way to communicate across distances in ancient Greece was by long distance runner. The most famous message in the history of ancient Greece was carried in 490 B.C. The Athenians were at war with the Persians. The two armies met at the Battle of Marathon. The Greeks won a great victory, and they sent a messenger running back to Athens to relay the news. The distance was about twenty-six miles, the same distance as a modern marathon, hence the name.

WHAT GODS DID THE GREEKS WORSHIP?

The religious beliefs of the ancient Greeks were of central importance in their lives. The Greeks believed that the gods they worshipped took an active interest in them and could interfere in their lives at any time. This belief meant that religion had a place in everything they did. The importance of religion in ancient Greek society is easy to see in the huge temples they built, many of which still stand today.

Ancient Greek religion was polytheistic. This term means that the ancient Greeks believed that there were many gods and goddesses. Each of these gods and goddesses had control over one aspect of the world. For example, Aphrodite was the goddess of love, Demeter was the goddess of the harvest, and Dionysus was the god of wine. All of these gods and goddesses were believed to be very much like mortal humans. They quarreled, fought with each other, played music, fell

Rituals and processions

What does it tell us?

Between 438 and 432 B.C., a frieze was added to the walls of the Parthenon. The frieze tells historians a lot about rituals in ancient Greece, particularly festival processions. This frieze portrays the procession of the sacred robe of Athena.

▲ This statue, from the 5th–4th century B.C., shows two of the most important Greek gods—Zeus and his wife, Hera, enthroned.

in love, married, and had children. For example, Athena, the goddess of art and wisdom, was the daughter of the god Zeus and the half-goddess Metis. All these gods and goddesses even had their own home. The ancient Greeks believed that their gods and goddesses lived at the top of Mount Olympus. This mountain is in the north of the country and is the highest point in Greece. The fact that gods and goddesses behaved like ordinary mortals meant that they did not always behave well. Therefore it was important to worship them properly so they would not be offended.

THE MAJOR GODS

The most important god living on Mount Olympus was Zeus. He was the god of the sky and the ruler of the other gods and goddesses. Greeks saw him as the main protector and ruler of the people of ancient Greece as well. He was also the god of rain, the clouds, and storms. Greek artists usually portrayed him as a kingly, bearded figure.

Greeks believed that the goddess Athena was born—fully grown and dressed in armor—by emerging from the head of her father, Zeus. The goddess of art, wisdom, mythology, industry, and war, Athena supported the Greeks besieging the city of Troy during the Trojan War. Greeks also believed she invented the plow, the flute, and shoemaking.

The Greeks usually portrayed Apollo as a beautiful young man. According to Greek myths, his father was Zeus, and he was the half-brother of Athena. Greeks held him to be the god of agriculture, cattle, light, and truth. Like Athena, he gave humans gifts, the most important of which was that of healing.

Clouds partially obscure this view of Mount Olympus, once believed to be the home of the gods and goddesses of ancient Greece. ▼

▲ An ancient Greek frieze from the fourth century B.C. showing Aesculapius, the Greek god of healing treating an arm injury in a sickroom

The Parthenon frieze

What does it tell us?

Within the Acropolis in Athens, a temple known as the Parthenon was dedicated to the goddess Athena. All four sides of the building were decorated with carvings known as friezes (*shown, in part, above*) illustrating ancient Greek religion and mythology. The friezes show us many details of Greek beliefs and styles of dress.

WORSHIPPING GODS

The center of worship for most ancient Greeks was a small altar in their homes. This usually would be found in the courtyard. The whole family, including any slaves, would worship together. Worship usually took the form of making some kind of burnt offering to the god or goddess they were praying to. This was intended as a kind of payment for the god or goddess to grant the family various favors.

Ancient Greeks also sacrificed animals, usually farm or domestic animals such as chickens and sheep. Outside of home altars, people built temples to many of the most important gods and goddesses, where large groups of people could worship together. The main shrine dedicated to Apollo was at a place called Delphi, which the Greeks believed was the center of the world. Athena's major temple, the Parthenon, was built on the Acropolis complex in Athens.

Important festivals took place every year, or every four years, at these shrines and temples. The most important festival, dedicated to Zeus, took place at Delphi. A priestess named Pythia would ask Zeus to predict the future.

MYTHS AND LEGENDS

Greek myths are mostly stories in which heroes had various adventures. In these myths, the gods and goddesses either helped the heroes or tried to get in their way. One of the most famous myths is the story of Jason and the Argonauts. Jason was sent on a journey to find and return an important object called the Golden Fleece. Along the way, Jason and the Argonauts faced many dangers but survived with the help of the goddesses Athena and Hera.

THE TEMPLES

Because religion played such a central part in the lives of all ancient Greeks, it

The temple of Athena Nike

What does it tell us?

The temple of Athena Nike was built in one corner of the Acropolis in Athens. It was built after the victory of the Athenians over the Persians in 480-479 B.C. This building shows us that the ancient Greeks built temples not just to worship a god or goddess but also to celebrate a great event that they believed the gods and goddesses helped bring about.

Temple of Ceres

What does it tell us?

Greek colonists in Sicily built the temple of Ceres (*shown here*) in the sixth century B.C. Many of the temples in Greece and other parts of the Mediterranean are not as well preserved. Swamps surrounded this temple, so very few people ever visited it. Because they are more complete, buildings like this help historians find out more about ancient Greek religion, building materials, and architectural styles.

is not surprising that the temples they built are among the largest and most imposing of all surviving ancient Greek structures.

It took many years for the Greeks to build these temples, and they used only the finest materials. Using carts, they transported large blocks of marble and carved them on site. They used stone and terra-cotta throughout the temples and, to complete and beautify the work, added sculptures and other decorations.

They made these great temples extremely large by creating columns to hold up the roofs. The Greeks used three different

column styles. The Doric style was a thick column with no decorations and no additional base stones. The Ionic and Corinthian styles each rested on a base of flat stones. The Ionic column was thinner, with a curved decoration capping the top. The Corinthian style was richly decorated, both along the sides of the column itself as well as on the top.

Image of Hercules on red pottery

What does it tell us?

The fact that many of the myths and legends of the ancient Greeks were represented in art shows how important these stories were. This vase (c. 600 B.C.) shows Hercules performing one of his legendary twelve tasks. Hercules was revered in ancient Greece as a man of great strength and courage who could do what seemed to be impossible tasks. A richly decorated piece of pottery such as this could only have been owned by somebody who was wealthy.

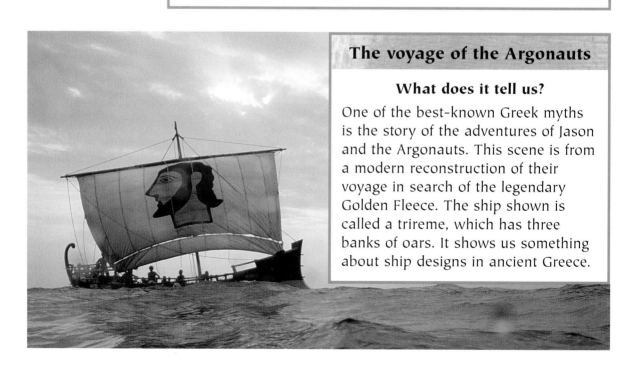

The voyage of the Argonauts

What does it tell us?

One of the best-known Greek myths is the story of the adventures of Jason and the Argonauts. This scene is from a modern reconstruction of their voyage in search of the legendary Golden Fleece. The ship shown is called a trireme, which has three banks of oars. It shows us something about ship designs in ancient Greece.

WHAT DID THE ANCIENT GREEKS CONTRIBUTE TO THE WORLD?

MODERN GREECE

In the two thousand years since the rise and fall of ancient Greek civilization, Greece has been ruled by many different foreign powers. These include ancient Rome, Byzantium, Spain, Italy, and France. From the fifteenth century on, Greece was dominated by its much more powerful Turkish neighbor. It was only in 1830 that Greece finally united and became an independent country. Today, Greece is part of a modern Europe and—with both the Olympics and the national football team winning the European championship in 2004—it is now seen as an important sports center.

SCIENCE AND MATHEMATICS

Many of the scientific and technological ideas that we take for granted today were first developed by the ancient Greeks. It was Aristharchus of Samos (310–250 B.C.) who first suggested that Earth revolved around the Sun. It was not until the seventeenth century, however, that this theory finally was proved.

The ancient Greeks also made advances in mathematics. In the sixth century B.C., two ancient Greek philosophers, Thales of Miletus (625–546 B.C.) and Pythagoras

This tile (c. A.D.1437–1439), from a building in Florence, Italy, shows Greek mathemeticians Euclid and Pythagorus at work. ▼

of Samos (582–500 B.C.), put forward the idea that the world could be explained not by the actions of gods, but by the principles of mathematics. Pythagoras was especially interested in geometry, the exploration of measuring area, volume, and length. He discovered that the three

angles inside a triangle always add up to 180 degrees. Without these mathematical discoveries, the calculations needed for modern building and engineering would be impossible. Much of the work of Pythagoras was taken further by Euclid (alive in about 300 B.C.). He discovered more about the properties of numbers and the mathematics of music.

HEALTH AND MEDICINE

As with many other ancient civilizations, progress in health and medicine in ancient Greece was held back by the fact that they did not know about the role germs and viruses play in disease. Many Greeks believed that disease was caused by gods who were punishing them. Therefore, the cure was to visit a temple, pray, and make a sacrifice.

By the sixth century B.C., however, Greek scientists began to believe that diseases also could be cured by using medicine or performing surgery. In the fifth century B.C., two medical schools opened at Kos and Cnidus. The most famous Greek physician was Hippocrates (460–377 B.C.). While it would be a long time until the role of germs in causing disease was understood, he believed that diseases were caused by nature and that it was the job of the doctor to help nature— through the use of medicine—cure the disease. His influence remains today, as every doctor must take the "Hippocratic

The Hippocratic oath

"I swear by Apollo the healer . . . I will employ treatments for the relief of suffering to the best of my ability and judgement."

What does it tell us?

Some historians believe that Hippocrates himself wrote this oath. It shows us that Hippocrates was turning medicine into a science and that doctors had to take an oath to protect their patients.

The seventeenth-century illustration below shows Hippocrates examining an animal skull.

Oath." This is a modern version of the oath taken by ancient Greek doctors, in which they promised to protect their patients and to— at the very least— "keep them from harm."

Statue of Socrates

What does it tell us?

The Greeks, and later the Romans, carved many statues of their great philosophers, mathematicians, and scientists. These statues show us how important they felt these people were in ancient Greece. Many modern scientists and mathematicians also recognize the great contributions made by them. This statue of Socrates, created between 1859 and 1885, stands outside the Hellenic Academy in Athens.

ARCHITECTURE

From about 1750 to the 1800s, Europe and the United States became very interested in the ancient Greeks. In painting and in sculpture, the style of the ancient Greeks was studied and copied. It was in the field of architecture, though, that the impact of the ancient Greeks became most noticeable in a new style called *neoclassical*. Many of the great eighteenth and nineteenth-century cities in Europe and North America constructed buildings inspired by the design of ancient Greek temples. In fact, Edinburgh, the capital of Scotland, has so many neoclassical buildings it is called the "Athens of the North." U.S. versions of neoclassicism include Federal, Classical Revival, and Jeffersonian styles.

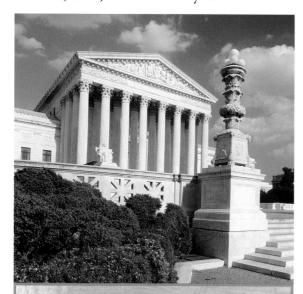

The Supreme Court Building

What does it tell us?

The U.S. Supreme Court Building, in Washington, D.C., was built between 1932 and 1935, less than one hundred years ago. It looks like an ancient Greek temple with Corinthian-style columns. It tells us that ancient Greek architecture still influences our own buildings. Ancient Greek law and politics also influenced the Founding Fathers of the United States of America. For example, the ancient Greeks taught them that all laws had to be written down and agreed to by the people who had to obey them.

THE FIRST DEMOCRACY

Today many of us live in democracies. This means that every adult has the chance to help decide who will run the government in his or her country for several years. This usually is done through a secret voting system. The Athenian system of government was not as democratic as modern democracies, mainly because women were not allowed to vote. This was, however, the first form of government in which the full participation of citizens in the running of a country was seen as a good thing rather than something dangerous.

▲ The ancient Acropolis still stands, with its temples towering over Athens. The temples are in the process of careful restoration.

Scene from the opening ceremony of the 2004 Olympics

What does it tell us?

The opening ceremony of the 2004 Olympics in Athens has been widely regarded as one of the most spectacular in the history of the modern Olympic movement. Ancient Greek mythology and history were an important part of the ceremony. Scenes from Greek myths played a central part in the ceremony. This tells us that modern Greeks are still strongly influenced by their ancient past and that they remain very proud of the achievements of their ancestors.

TIME LINE

FIND OUT MORE

B.C.	**1200**	Destruction of ancient Mycenaean civilization
	740	First Greek writing emerges
	735–700	First Greek colonies founded in Sicily
	776	First Olympic Games held
	600–500	Earliest written laws created
	490	Athenians defeat Persians at Battle of Marathon
	490–479	War with Persians
	480	Persians destroy Acropolis
	468	First play, written by Sophocles, performed with three actors
	447–432	Major improvements to Acropolis
	438	Consecration of Parthenon
	431–405	War between Sparta and Athens
	359	Philip II, father of Alexander the Great, becomes king of Macedonia
	356	Birth of Alexander the Great
	338	Philip II defeats Athenians and Thebans, making Macedonia the most powerful state in Greece
	337	Alexander the Great becomes king of Macedonia and rules Greece
	334–333	Alexander the Great attacks and vanquishes the Persians
	327	Alexander controls much of present-day Central Asia
	323	Death of Alexander the Great begins the Hellenistic Age, when Greek culture dominated much of eastern Mediterranean and the Middle East
A.D.	**146**	Greece conquered by the Romans

Books

Bendick, Jeanne. *Archimedes and the Door to Science.* Bethlehem Books, 1995.

Chrisp, Peter. *Alexander the Great.* Dorling Kindersley Publishing, 2000.

James, John and Louise James. *The Greeks.* Bedrick, 2002.

Oberman ,Sheldon. *Island of the Minotaur: Greek Myths of Ancient Crete.* Crocodile Books, 2003.

Tames, Richard. *Ancient Greek Children.* People in the Past (series). Heinemann, 2002.

Zannos, Susan. *The Life and Times of Socrates.* Biography from Ancient Civilizations (series). Mitchell Lane Publishers, 2004.

Web Sites

www.ancientgreece.com/
Explore ancient Greek life.

www.bbc.co.uk/schools/ancientgreece
Discover information and activities for ancient Greece, with materials for teachers and parents.

gogreece.about.com/cs/mythology/a/mythaphrodite.htm
Learn more about Greek mythology, gods, and goddesses with this well-organized site.

www.ancient-greece.co.uk/
Enjoy interactive ancient Greek displays using the huge collections of the British Museum.

GLOSSARY

Amphidromia—child-welcoming ceremony for newborns in ancient Greece

andron—small dining area where men would entertain their friends, usually located on the north side of the home

ariston—the first meal of the day, the light midday meal of ancient Athens

artifacts physical products made by humans that remain from a particular period in a culture's history and represent that culture

Assembly—a gathering of citizens in Athens who would make decisions about how Athens was run

chiton—most common form of clothing for both men and women in ancient Greece: a long belted covering, made of linen, with loose sleeves that were held in place with pins

city-state—an independent city that controls the territory, or state, that surrounds it

Corinthian—one of the three styles of Greek architecture, having the most highly decorated columns

council—governing body of twenty-eight nobles, which controlled the business of the Assembly

deipnon—the second and main meal of the day, the evening meal in ancient Athens

Doric—the simplest and oldest of the three styles of Greek architecture, characterized by Doric columns, which are thick and have no decorations or separate base

ephors—men who belonged to the ephorate of Sparta, which ruled Sparta's government

grammatistes—ancient Greek name for teachers

greaves—leg guards for Greek soldiers

gynaeceum—area in the house set aside for women, usually located at the back of the home

himation—cloak worn over a chiton

hippodrome—an oval stadium used for chariot and horse races

hoplite—Greek foot soldier, who was typically heavily protected with a helmet, breastplate, and greaves while carrying a hardwood shield in his left hand, spear in his right, and wearing a sword at his side

Ionic—one of three styles of Greek architecture, whose columns are characterized by their stylized caps, which have a curl on either side of their flat tops

orchestra—in ancient Greece, the circular stage on which a drama took place

peplos—an early, sleeveless version of the chiton, made of heavy wool that was belted at the waist and fastened at each shoulder with a large pin

polytheism—belief in more than one god. The ancient Greeks believed in many gods and goddesses and created many dramatic stories, or myths, about them

symposium—a drinking party to which men would invite their male friends

theatron—the seating area for the audience in an ancient Greek theater

INDEX